# COUNTDOWN TO SPACE

# NEIL ARMSTRONG
## A Space Biography

## Carmen Bredeson

Series Advisor:
John E. McLeaish
Chief, Public Information Office, retired,
NASA Johnson Space Center

**Enslow Publishers, Inc.**

| | |
|---|---|
| 44 Fadem Road | PO Box 38 |
| Box 699 | Aldershot |
| Springfield, NJ 07081 | Hants GU12 6BP |
| USA | UK |

**Library of Congress Cataloging-in-Publication Data**

Bredeson, Carmen.
    Neil Armstrong : a space biography / Carmen Bredeson.
       p. cm. — (Countdown to space)
    Includes bibliographical references and index.
    Summary: A biography of the first man on the moon, covering his youth, his career as an astronaut, and his life after NASA.
    ISBN 0-89490-973-8
    1. Armstrong, Neil, 1930–   —Juvenile literature. 2. Astronauts—United States—Biography—Juvenile literature. [1. Armstrong, Neil, 1930–
2. Astronauts.]  I. Title. II. Series.
TL789.85.A75B74  1998
629.45'0092—dc21
[B]                                           97-25449
                                               CIP
                                               AC

Printed in the United States of America

10 9 8 7 6 5 4 3 2 1

**Illustration Credits:** Library of Congress, pp. 15, 16, 22, 24; National Aeronautics and Space Administration (NASA), pp. 4, 6, 8, 10, 11, 20, 25, 28, 30, 32, 37, 38, 39, 40; National Archives, p. 14.

**Cover Illustration:** National Aeronautics and Space Administration (NASA) (foreground); Raghvendra Sahai and John Trauger (JPL), the WFPC2 science team, NASA, and AURA/STSCI (background).

# CONTENTS

*A technician works atop the white room, at right, through which the Apollo 11 astronauts entered the Columbia spacecraft.*

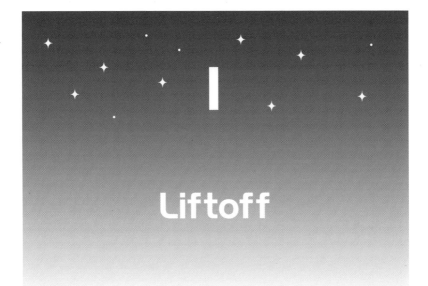

# Liftoff

The big day had finally arrived! Astronauts Neil Armstrong, Michael Collins, and Edwin "Buzz" Aldrin were ready to go to the Moon. After waking up at 4:00 A.M., the three sat down for a breakfast of steak, scrambled eggs, toast, orange juice, and coffee. Once they had eaten, the astronauts began the slow process of suiting up. When all the tubes and wires were connected just right, the trio got into an elevator for a ride up to the command module. *Columbia* was perched 400 feet in the air, on top of a huge Saturn V rocket.

Neil Armstrong later said: "As we ascended in the elevator to the top of the Saturn on the morning of July 16, 1969, we knew that hundreds of thousands of

Americans had given their best effort to give us this chance. Now it was time for us to give our best."[1]

While the astronauts were being strapped into their seats aboard *Columbia*, excitement filled the beaches and roads around Cape Canaveral, Florida. Nearly a million people had come to watch the liftoff of *Apollo 11.* Some camped in tents; others sat in lawn chairs and on the tops of cars. Out on the water, hundreds of boats bobbed in the sunshine. They were all there for just one thing. They wanted to see history being made. If all went as planned, Neil Armstrong and Buzz Aldrin

*Thousands of people spent the night before the* Apollo 11 *launch in tents, campers, cars, and on the beaches next to the Kennedy Space Center.*

would be the first human beings to set foot on the Moon.

At 9:32 A.M., the crowd heard a low rumble. It was followed by an ear-shattering roar. As the enormous Saturn V rocket lifted off from launchpad 39-A, smoke and flames belched from its engines. On the ground, many cheered and clapped, while others dropped to their knees and prayed for the brave astronauts. Onboard one of the boats, Janet Armstrong watched as her husband, Neil, embarked on one of mankind's greatest adventures. Gazing into the sky with her were the couple's sons—Eric, age twelve, and Mark, age six. Years later, Eric said, "It never occurred to me that it wouldn't work."[2]

Eleven minutes after liftoff, *Columbia* entered Earth orbit, traveling at a speed of more than 17,000 miles per hour. Neil Armstrong radioed Mission Control: "Hey, Houston, *Apollo 11*. This Saturn gave us a magnificent ride. We have no complaints with any of the three stages on that ride. It was beautiful."[3] After going around Earth one and a half times, the Saturn's rockets were fired again. The boost sent *Columbia*'s speed up to more than 24,000 miles per hour, fast enough to escape Earth orbit.

For three days, the astronauts raced through the blackness of space on their quarter-of-a-million-mile trip to the Moon. They did routine chores, ate, and tried to get some extra sleep. Some of their time was spent doing television interviews. Those watching the broadcasts on

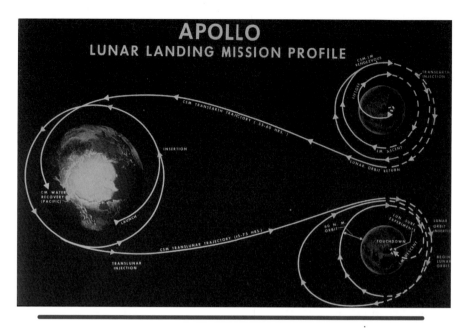

*The* Apollo 11 *flight plan diagram shows the launch pattern of* Columbia, *around Earth and into the Moon's orbit. To return from the Moon, the crew inside* Columbia *needed to first orbit the Moon and then travel back to Earth.*

Earth got a look at the inside of the command module, where the astronauts lived. On the fourth day of its space journey, *Columbia* flew past the western edge of the Moon. Lunar gravity captured the spacecraft and pulled it into orbit.

On the morning of Sunday, July 20, the relaxed atmosphere inside *Columbia* changed. This was the day that Neil Armstrong and Buzz Aldrin were scheduled to land on the Moon. After a quick breakfast, the crew got to work. Armstrong and Aldrin crawled through the tunnel that connected *Columbia* with *Eagle*. *Eagle* was the lunar module, or LM, that would carry the astronauts to the Moon's surface. Behind them, Michael Collins closed the hatches and unplugged the wires that connected the two spacecraft.

From inside *Columbia*, Collins said, "I have five minutes and fifteen seconds since we started. Attitude is holding very well." Aldrin answered from *Eagle*, "Roger, Mike, just hold it a little longer." Collins replied, "No sweat, I can hold it all day. Take your sweet time."[4] Inside *Eagle*, Armstrong and Aldrin checked all the instruments one more time. Just before the spacecraft disappeared behind the Moon on its thirteenth orbit, Mission Control radioed: "We're go for undocking."[5]

The astronauts were behind the Moon and out of radio contact with Mission Control for thirty-three minutes. The Moon has no atmosphere for radio waves to bounce from and reach Earth. *Columbia* and *Eagle* still had radio contact with each other, though. Just before the two ships separated, Michael Collins said, "You cats take it easy on the lunar surface. . . ." Buzz Aldrin answered, "OK, Mike."[6] Then Collins threw the switch that disconnected the ships.

As *Eagle* pulled away from *Columbia*, Neil Armstrong said, "The *Eagle* has wings." Collins replied, "It doesn't look like any eagle I have ever seen. It is the weirdest-looking contraption ever to invade the sky."[7] *Eagle* did indeed look like a big metallic bug with its four spindly legs and shimmering gold color.

*After the lunar module (LM) disconnected from the command module, it began its descent to the Moon's surface. Inside, Neil Armstrong and Buzz Aldrin were on their way to making history.*

Communications were finally restored between Earth and the astronauts. The engineers and scientists in Houston were relieved to learn that the separation of *Columbia* and *Eagle* had been successful. Mission Control radioed that the time had arrived for the LM to actually descend to the Moon's surface. *"Eagle,* Houston. If you read, you're GO for powered descent." "Roger," Armstrong replied.[8]

Flames shot out of the bottom of the LM while an

engine powered it toward the surface of the Moon. Closer and closer it got until Neil Armstrong realized that they were headed right for a crater filled with huge rocks. He said, "I had an excellent view of the crater and the boulder field out of the left window. There were boulders big as Volkswagens strewn all around. The rocks seemed to be coming up at us awfully fast."[9]

Rather than risk crashing into a boulder, Armstrong took over manual control of the landing with only ninety seconds of fuel left. There was plenty of fuel for takeoff, but that could only be used to get *Eagle* back off the Moon. The two fuel systems were separate. With

*As Neil Armstrong approached the Moon's surface in* Eagle, *he needed to think quickly and steer* Eagle *away from a field of boulders.* Eagle's *shadow can be seen in the lower left corner.*

time running out, Armstrong peered out a small window. He scanned the surface, looking for a safe place to land. If *Eagle* ran out of fuel, it would crash. Armstrong had to find a place to land right away or the mission would be aborted.

As *Eagle* skimmed the surface of the Moon, the fuel level dropped lower and lower. Ninety seconds' worth of fuel quickly became sixty seconds' worth and then forty-five. Buzz Aldrin had his hand on the Abort Stage button as *Eagle* hovered seventy-five feet above the lunar surface. As the LM descended, it began kicking up clouds of lunar dust.

Houston: Thirty seconds [of fuel remaining].

*Eagle*: Contact light! OK, engine stop.

Houston: We copy you down, *Eagle*.

*Eagle*: Houston, Tranquility Base here. The *Eagle* has landed.

Houston: Roger, Tranquility. We copy you on the ground. You've got a bunch of guys about to turn blue. We're breathing again. Thanks a lot.[10]

With only eighteen seconds of fuel reserves left, *Eagle* and its crew were finally on the lunar surface. In a few short hours, Neil Armstrong was scheduled to climb down a ladder and become the first man on the Moon. What events in his past prepared him for this amazing feat?

# 2

# Preparing for Space

Neil Armstrong was born on August 5, 1930, the oldest of Stephen and Viola Armstrong's three children. When he was just six years old, Neil took his first airplane ride. The short trip in an old Ford trimotor hooked the future astronaut on flying. Aviation magazines filled the shelves in Neil's room, along with airplane models that he built in his spare time.

When Neil was fourteen, he decided that he wanted to take flying lessons. There was an airfield outside of his hometown of Wapakoneta, Ohio. Flying lessons were expensive, though, at nine dollars an hour. To pay for the lessons, Neil worked in a local drugstore before and after school for forty cents an hour. It took a lot of

*At the age of six, Neil Armstrong took a trip on a Ford trimotor airplane, similar to the one shown. This sparked young Neil's interest in flying.*

hours of lifting cartons and sweeping the floor to save the money for one lesson.

When he had enough money saved, Neil jumped on his bike and pedaled the three miles to Wapak Flying Service. He got his pilot's license on August 5, 1946, the day of his sixteenth birthday, after taking lessons for two years. He could fly a plane all by himself even though he did not have a license to drive a car yet! One of Neil's high school teachers said, "He always had a goal to work on."[1]

All of Neil's hours were not involved with flying. He was also active in the Boy Scouts. During his first year of college, Neil made Eagle Scout. While he was attending Wapakoneta High School, he played baritone horn in a jazz combo he formed. As the day of his high school graduation drew near in 1947, he began to apply to colleges. The day he got a Navy scholarship to Purdue University, he raced home to tell his mother. She got so excited that she dropped a jar of preserves on her foot and broke a toe!

In the fall of 1947, Neil Armstrong began college at Purdue University, located in West Lafayette, Indiana. He enrolled in the department of aeronautical engineering and joined the Naval Air Cadet program. After two years at Purdue, Armstrong was called into active duty in the Navy. He completed flight training at Pensacola, Florida, and was sent to fight in the Korean War. Armstrong flew seventy-eight missions as a Navy fighter pilot.

During one of Neil Armstrong's missions, his jet's wingtip was sheared off when the plane hit a wire. The wire had been stretched across a valley by the North

*Stephen and Viola Armstrong became the proud parents of the first man to walk on the Moon.*

Koreans to trap low-flying aircraft. Armstrong managed to fly the damaged aircraft back to a safe landing. For his bravery in several air battles, he was awarded three Air Medals.

With his tour of duty over in 1952, Neil Armstrong returned to Purdue to finish his education. Often, when he was walking to his classes, he saw a fellow student named Janet Shearon. They sometimes stopped to talk, but Neil did not ask her for a date for several months. She later said, "He is not one to rush into anything."[2]

As a test pilot, Neil Armstrong (top left) flew experimental planes for the United States government. He is shown here at Miramar Naval Air Station in San Diego, California, with other X-15 test pilots.

Neil Armstrong graduated from Purdue in 1955, and the couple married the following year.

After graduation, Armstrong naturally gravitated to a career that involved flying. He went to work as a test pilot for the National Advisory Committee for Aeronautics. For seven years, he flew experimental planes for the United States government. He logged more than one thousand hours in aircraft such as the X-15 rocket plane. Once, while flying the X-15, Armstrong set a record. He reached an altitude of 207,500 feet at a speed of 3,989 miles per hour.[3] One of his friends said, "He flies an airplane like he's wearing it."[4]

# 3

# The Race for Space

While Neil Armstrong was busy risking his life in experimental airplanes, the United States was gearing up for the space race. On October 4, 1957, the Soviet Union stunned the world when it launched *Sputnik 1*. The 184-pound, beach ball-sized satellite was the first man-made object launched into Earth's orbit. The United States shifted into high gear to try to catch up with the Soviets. Nearly four months later, the United States successfully launched a bullet-shaped satellite called *Explorer 1*. The space race was on, and the goal of both countries was to be the first to put a human being into space.

The National Aeronautics and Space Administration (NASA) was created in 1958. Soon after, America's first seven astronauts were selected from a group of 110 military test pilots. Neil Armstrong did not apply to be part of this first group of space pioneers. The new astronauts were called the Mercury 7 after the Mercury spacecraft they would fly. The seven men became heroes after their names were announced on April 9, 1959. They were seen as brave men ". . . who would dare to ride the rockets that so often exploded in raging fireballs over Cape Canaveral."[1]

Alan Shepard was chosen from among the Mercury 7 to be the first American in space. Just one month before Shepard's scheduled flight, Soviet cosmonaut Yuri Gagarin was launched into orbit aboard *Vostok 1*. After the Soviet surprise, astronaut John Glenn said, "They just beat the pants off us, that's all. . . . But now that the space age has begun, there's going to be plenty of work for everybody."[2]

On May 5, 1961, Alan Shepard became the first American in space. Twenty days after Shepard's successful fifteen-minute flight, President John F. Kennedy said to the members of Congress, "I believe that this nation should commit itself to achieving the goal, before this decade is out, of landing a man on the Moon and returning him safely to Earth."[3]

In order to meet Kennedy's incredible challenge, NASA needed more room. Construction of a new Mission Control Center and Astronaut Training Facility was started in 1961. The 1,620-acre site was located

*Even before Neil Armstrong became an astronaut, President John F. Kennedy announced that the United States should work to land a man on the Moon by 1970. That man would turn out to be Neil Armstrong.*

twenty-five miles southeast of downtown Houston, Texas. All flights would be controlled from the Manned Space Center, but the spacecraft would still be launched from Cape Canaveral, Florida.

NASA's first flights in preparation for a Moon landing were called Project Mercury. From 1961 until 1963, six manned flights lifted off. The successful missions proved that human beings could be launched into orbit, survive in space, and be recovered safely. Each flight was a little longer and more complicated than the one before. At the end of Project Mercury, NASA was ready to move on to the next phase, Project Gemini.

Since the Gemini spacecraft held two men, more astronauts were needed. By this time, Neil Armstrong had enough hours as a test pilot to qualify for the job. He was one of two hundred applicants for the nine positions. In September 1962, Armstrong was selected to be one of NASA's new astronauts. He and his wife packed their belongings and moved from California to Texas with their five-year-old son, Eric. Another son, Mark, was born shortly after they arrived in Houston. (The Armstrongs were also the parents of a daughter who died in 1962 when she was two years old.)

Neil Armstrong's training included hundreds of hours in flight simulators, learning just which buttons to push and what levers to pull. He was whirled around in a giant centrifuge to experience the g-forces he would feel during liftoff and reentry. A g-force is the pressure that the body feels when the spacecraft changes speed or direction quickly. Armstrong also listened to lectures about astronomy and rocket propulsion.

Two unmanned and ten manned Gemini flights were flown between 1964 and 1966. During the missions, astronauts learned how to do the things that would make a trip to the Moon possible. On *Gemini 4*, Edward

White took the first United States space walk and learned what it was like to try to move around in the vacuum of space. The eight-day *Gemini 5* flight proved that human beings could survive in space for extended periods.

Space rendezvous was practiced during *Gemini 6* and 7. Spacecraft needed to rendezvous, or closely approach each other, prior to connecting. Astronauts on

the Moon had to be able to launch the LM into the path of the command module. The LM was not capable of returning to Earth on its own. It had to dock with the command module for the return trip. Therefore, docking also had to be practiced. Astronauts Neil Armstrong and David Scott were chosen to attempt the first docking on *Gemini 8*. It would be Armstrong's first trip into space.

*As an astronaut in training, Armstrong listened to science lectures. On March 16, 1966, Armstrong would put his training to good use as he and David Scott attempted the first docking in space.*

# 4

# Emergencies

On the morning of March 16, 1966, an Agena target satellite blasted off from Cape Canaveral's launchpad 14 at 10:00 A.M. Forty minutes later, Neil Armstrong and David Scott were hurled into space from launchpad 19 for their three-day flight. For the first time in history, two spacecraft would attempt to dock, or connect, in flight. Five hours after liftoff, *Gemini 8* caught up with the Agena satellite. After inspecting their target carefully, the astronauts aboard *Gemini 8* eased its nose into the docking port on the Agena. As the connection clicked into place, Armstrong said: "Flight, we are docked. It's really a smoothie. No noticeable oscillation [swinging] at all."[1]

With the Agena and *Gemini 8* still hooked together,

*Neil Armstrong wears a wide grin prior to his Gemini 8 launch. A suit technician makes final adjustments to Armstrong's space suit during the dressing operation.*

Armstrong started to steer the two vehicles into a higher orbit. They were flying almost two hundred miles above China and were out of radio contact with the ground. Thirty minutes after docking, the two spacecraft suddenly started to tumble end over end. Faster and faster they went. Neil Armstrong wrestled with the controls. Nothing he did seemed to stop the tumbling. Inside *Gemini 8*, the astronauts were getting dizzy.

In an effort to save the spacecraft and their lives, Armstrong unlocked *Gemini 8* from the Agena. Instead of solving the problem, the capsule started tumbling even faster. It was making a complete turn every second. The astronauts were nearly unconscious. A tracking ship in the Pacific Ocean picked up a message from Armstrong that said, "We have a serious problem here. . . . We're tumbling end over end up here."[2]

Somehow the spacecraft had to be stabilized before both astronauts passed out. Neil Armstrong threw the rules away and shut down the sixteen thrusters that were used to maneuver the capsule. He then switched on the nose rocket thrusters that were used during reentry. For thirty minutes, he blasted away on those thrusters until he regained control of *Gemini 8* and stopped the tumbling.

*Blastoff of the Titan booster rocket (left) lifted Neil Armstrong and David Scott into space inside the* Gemini 8 *capsule. They were on their way to attempt the first docking of two spacecraft—their* Gemini 8 *capsule with an Agena satellite (right), which had blasted into space forty minutes earlier.*

Mission Control ordered an emergency landing in the western Pacific. Although the astronauts did not have tracking stations to give them location reports, their reentry was right on target. They splashed down 480 miles east of Okinawa, ten hours and forty-one minutes after liftoff. They were picked up by a recovery team and were safe aboard a Navy destroyer three hours after splashdown.

A monthlong examination of *Gemini 8* showed that thruster number eight had jammed open at full power. An electrical short had apparently caused the problem. With the thruster stuck open and spewing fuel into space, the delicate balance of the capsule was destroyed. By shutting down the thrusters, Neil Armstrong had saved *Gemini 8* from disaster. NASA flight director Chris Kraft said, "That was truly a fantastic recovery by a human being under such circumstances and really proved why we have test pilots in those ships. Had it not been for that good flying, we probably would have lost that crew."[3]

By the time of the last Gemini flight in 1966, NASA officials were ready to shoot for the Moon. However, there were many steps to take before a lunar landing was possible. First the three-man Apollo spacecraft had to be tested to see if it was safe. On January 27, 1967, *Apollo 1* astronauts were in their command module, conducting a mock countdown of the flight.

At T minus ten minutes in the countdown, someone

suddenly shouted, "Fire in the spacecraft!"[4] Within minutes, astronauts Gus Grissom, Ed White, and Roger Chaffee were dead. Six minutes after the fire started, the ground crew pried off the hatch of *Apollo 1*. Astronaut Deke Slayton said:

> It was devastating. Everything inside was burned, black with ash. It was a death chamber. The crew had obviously been trying to get out. The three bodies were piled in front of the seal in the hatch. Ed White was on the bottom and Gus and Roger were crumpled on top of him.[5]

The tragedy of *Apollo 1* nearly finished NASA's plans to go to the Moon. Two years of investigation followed the fire. Every part of the capsule was examined in detail. Each procedure was reviewed again and again. In the end, a short circuit in a wire near Grissom's seat was blamed for the tragedy. During the two years, more than one thousand changes were made in the command module. It took the work of about 150,000 men and women to get the program back on track. Three unmanned and four manned Apollo missions were flown from November 1967 to May 1969. They tested the capsule and the lunar lander and orbited the Moon several times.

While testing a Lunar Landing Research Vehicle (LLRV) here on Earth, Neil Armstrong was nearly killed. He was flying the wingless, jet- and rocket-powered craft at Ellington Air Force Base in Houston on May 6, 1968.

During landing, when he was just two hundred feet off the ground, the craft started to shake and backfire. As smoke poured from the engine, the LLRV rolled over and began falling toward the ground. Just before crashing, Armstrong pulled the eject handle. As the LLRV exploded into flames, Armstrong parachuted to safety. He later said, "The only damage to me was that I bit my tongue."[6]

With that near disaster behind him, it was finally time for the moment of truth. *Apollo 11* was scheduled to lift off in the summer of 1969 and land the first man on the Moon. Flying aboard the spacecraft would be Neil Armstrong, Edwin "Buzz" Aldrin, and Michael Collins. They were selected to fly on the mission because they were next in line on the crew list. As it turned out, they were about to make history.

*Neil Armstrong's parachute floats him safely to the ground after a Lunar Landing Research Vehicle crashes and burns. Armstrong was practicing a Moon landing. This photograph is an enlargement of a documentary film clip made during the event.*

# 5

# Moon Walk

It was July 20, 1969, eight years after President John F. Kennedy had challenged America to put a man on the Moon. Astronauts Neil Armstrong and Buzz Aldrin sat safely in *Eagle* on the surface of the Moon. Overhead, Michael Collins orbited in *Columbia.*

A four-hour rest period was scheduled for the astronauts. Because of their excitement, they requested that the rest period be canceled. Mission Control agreed, and the men began to put on their bulky space suits in the close quarters of the LM.

Temperatures on the Moon soar to over 120°C (250°F) during the day and fall to below -150°C (-250°F) at night. There is no oxygen to breathe or water to drink. The 160-pound space suits that the astronauts wore contained life-support systems that kept the oxygen flowing and temperature comfortable. There was also a straw built into the helmets so that the men could drink water when they got thirsty. Communications equipment allowed them to talk to each other and to Mission Control on Earth.

With their suits in place, Armstrong and Aldrin opened *Eagle*'s hatch. A camera mounted on the outside of the LM sent fuzzy black-and-white pictures back to Earth. Half a billion people from all over the world were

*Astronaut Buzz Aldrin makes his way down the ladder to set foot on the Moon. Fifteen minutes earlier, Neil Armstrong had become the first human to touch the lunar surface.*

glued to their television sets. They were barely breathing as Neil Armstrong made his way down the ladder. One clumsy step at a time, he gradually neared the ladder's bottom rung. Finally, he hopped the last three and a half feet to the lunar surface. As his feet hit, he became the first human being ever to set foot on the Moon. He said: "That's one small step for a man, one giant leap for mankind."[1]

Back home, people began breathing again as they watched Armstrong take his first steps on the Moon. Buzz Aldrin joined his fellow astronaut fifteen minutes later. The men had a great deal of work to do. The first visit to the lunar surface was short because scientists were not sure how human beings would react to being on the Moon. In the two hours that they were allowed, the astronauts had to set up several scientific experiments. They also had to gather two containers of lunar soil and rocks and put up an American flag. Neil Armstrong later said, "The primary difficulty was just far too little time to do a variety of things we would have liked. We had the problem of the five-year-old boy in a candy store."[2]

As the astronauts gathered their samples, they described conditions on the Moon to the viewers back home. Neil Armstrong said, "The surface is fine and powdery, it adheres in fine layers, like powdered charcoal, to the soles and sides of my foot."[3] The men did not seem to have any trouble walking on the Moon.

They said it felt as though they were floating. In their space suits, they would have weighed about 360 pounds each on Earth. The Moon has only one-sixth the gravity of Earth, though. Each astronaut and his suit weighed only 60 pounds on the lunar surface.

About an hour into the Moon walk, Neil Armstrong and Buzz Aldrin received a phone call from President Richard Nixon. He said, "Neil and Buzz, I am talking to

you by telephone from the Oval Office at the White House, and this certainly has to be the most historic telephone call ever made. . . . Because of what you have done, the heavens have become a part of man's world." Armstrong replied, "It's a great honor and privilege for us to be here, representing not only the United States but men of peace of all nations, and with interest and a curiosity and a vision for the future."[4]

*In their two hours on the Moon's surface, the astronauts set up experiments and collected samples of lunar soil and rocks.*

The two-hour Moon walk was over much too soon. Just before the men returned to *Eagle*, they uncovered a metal plaque that was attached to one of the LM's legs. It read: "Here men from the planet Earth first set foot upon the Moon, July 1969, A.D. We came in peace for all mankind."[5]

With that last task completed, the astronauts gathered up their precious cargo of Moon rocks, climbed into *Eagle*, and closed the hatch. Once inside, they pressurized the cabin, removed their space suits, and settled down for a scheduled five-hour rest. Sleep was nearly impossible in the cold, cramped cabin of the LM. Both men put their helmets back on to keep from breathing the lunar dust that filled the cabin.

Finally, twenty-one hours after touchdown, it was time for *Eagle* to blast off and rendezvous with *Columbia* and Michael Collins. While the engineers waited nervously in Mission Control, Neil Armstrong powered up the LM's ascent engine. If it failed to start, *Eagle* would be stranded on the Moon. Too short an engine burn would send the LM crashing back to the lunar surface. This part of the system had never been tested on Earth because it was designed to work only in the Moon's low gravity.

All systems worked perfectly. The bottom part of the LM served as a launchpad as *Eagle* lifted off in a cloud of lunar dust. Three hours and ten minutes later, *Eagle* docked with *Columbia*, which had been circling sixty-nine miles above the lunar surface. Neil Armstrong and Buzz Aldrin crawled through the tunnel, opened the hatch, and entered *Columbia*. Michael Collins described their reunion:

> The first one through is Buzz, with a big smile on his face. I grab his head, a hand on each temple, and am about to give him a smooch on the forehead, as a parent might greet an errant child; but then, embarrassed, I think better of it and grab his hand, and then Neil's. We cavort about a little bit, all smiles and giggles over our success, and then it's back to work as usual.[6]

The *Apollo 11* astronauts fired up *Columbia*'s main engine and began their sixty-hour trip back to Earth. In the space capsule with them were forty-seven pounds of lunar samples, sealed in two vacuum-tight metal containers. During their last evening in space before splashdown, Neil Armstrong said to those listening on Earth:

> We would like to give special thanks to all those Americans who built the spacecraft. . . . To these people tonight, we give a special thank you, and to all the other people that are listening and watching tonight, God bless you. Good night from *Apollo 11*.[7]

# 6

# Splashdown

On July 24, 1969, *Columbia* splashed down in the Pacific Ocean, 950 miles southwest of Hawaii. The U.S.S. *Hornet* and its crew were ready and waiting for the astronauts. It was possible that the *Apollo 11* crew had picked up some deadly microbes on the lunar surface. To keep any unknown lunar organisms from spreading to those on Earth, many precautions were taken with the recovery.

Several Navy divers jumped into the ocean to attach a flotation collar around *Columbia*. The men were dressed in biological insulation suits for protection. Three identical suits were quickly tossed into the hatch of *Columbia* for the astronauts to wear. Once in the suits, the astronauts stepped from the space capsule into a raft full of antiseptic. Additional antiseptic was sprayed around the closed hatch cover and on the outside of the astronauts' suits. Filters cleaned the air the men exhaled before it was released into the atmosphere.

Helicopters carried the crew to the deck of the aircraft carrier. Once there, the *Apollo 11* astronauts were quickly put into a quarantine van that was sealed. Inside were a doctor and a technician who would carefully monitor the men's health. The van had a large glass window in the rear so that the crew could communicate with the outside world. President Richard Nixon, who was aboard the carrier to greet the astronauts, said, "And I only hope that all of us in Government . . . can do our job a little better. We can reach for the stars, just as you have reached so far for the stars."[1]

The carrier made its way to Hawaii, where the van was moved into the hold of a C-141 cargo plane bound for Houston. Once there, the occupants of the van walked through an airtight tunnel into an isolation unit at NASA's Lunar Receiving Laboratory. Inside was a cook, along with several more doctors and technicians. Each had volunteered to spend the eighteen-day quarantine with the astronauts. No physical contact was allowed with anyone on the outside. The astronauts were able to use the phones freely to talk to their family and friends.

*After returning from the Moon, quarantined astronauts Neil Armstrong, Buzz Aldrin, and Michael Collins peek at the outside world.*

While the astronauts were being transported to Houston, the Moon rocks were also on their way to NASA. The containers were loaded into two separate airplanes in case of an accident. After their arrival in Houston, the samples were taken to the Lunar Receiving Laboratory. There they were placed in nitrogen-filled vacuum chambers and carefully opened and photographed.

Because the rocks might also harbor some deadly plague, NASA conducted a number of experiments on them. Germ-free mice were exposed to the material, along with houseflies and cockroaches. After three weeks of testing, the lunar samples were declared free of any strange Moon germs. Scientists from around the world were invited to study the material.

The Moon rocks were kept isolated and protected even after their quarantine period was over. Not so for the astronauts! Once they were found to be free of dangerous germs, they were able to join their families and friends. When they were finally released on August 11, 1969, they were greeted as heroes by an adoring public.

Neil Armstrong, Buzz Aldrin, and Michael Collins were given a ticker tape parade in New York City and invited to address Congress in Washington, D.C.

Receptions were also held in some of America's largest cities. All fifty state governors gathered in Los Angeles for a dinner honoring the *Apollo 11* astronauts.

Eventually, the excitement died down and the astronauts were able to get back to work at NASA. There were six more missions to

*Dr. Eugene Shoemaker (left) of the United States Geological Survey and Dr. William Kemmerer (right) of NASA examine a Moon rock at the Smithsonian Institution.*

*The city of Chicago welcomes the three NASA heroes—Neil Armstrong, Michael Collins, and Buzz Aldrin.*

the Moon. The crew of *Apollo 11* spent much of their time helping the next Apollo crews get ready for their trips. Neil Armstrong also served as the deputy associate administrator for aeronautics at NASA for two years after *Apollo 11.*

Then, in 1971, Armstrong retired from the space agency. He returned to Ohio and became a professor of aerospace engineering at the University of Cincinnati. He taught there until 1979. Since that time, he has been a computer company executive, has worked for an oil equipment firm, and has narrated television specials about aviation. Today, he is retired and lives with his

*Mayor John Lindsay awards the New York City Medal of Honor to* Apollo 11 *Commander Neil A. Armstrong on August 13, 1969.*

wife on a farm in Lebanon, Ohio, one hundred miles from his boyhood home. He rarely grants interviews and lives a very private life.

During the summer of 1994, there were many celebrations marking the twenty-fifth anniversary of *Apollo 11*. Neil Armstrong made several rare public appearances at some of those celebrations. A quarter of a century after his historic journey, Neil Armstrong wrote:

> Luna is once again isolated. Two decades have passed without footfalls on its dusty surface. No wheeled rovers patrol the lunar highlands. Silent ramparts guard vast territories never yet visited by man. Unseen vistas await the return of explorers from Earth. And they will return.[2]

# CHRONOLOGY

1930—Born on August 5 on a farm near Wapakoneta, Ohio.

1946—Received pilot's license on sixteenth birthday.

1947—Graduated from Wapakoneta High School; enrolled at Purdue University; joined Naval Air Cadet program.

1949—Called into active duty in the United States Navy.

1955—Graduated from Purdue University with a B.S. degree in aeronautical engineering.

1956—Married Janet Shearon.

1957—Son Eric born.

1957—Flew experimental aircraft for the United States
-1962 government.

1959—Daughter Karen born.

1962—Accepted into NASA's astronaut training program; daughter Karen died.

1963—Son Mark born.

1966—Flew aboard *Gemini 8* on March 16.

1969—Lifted off in *Apollo 11* on July 16; became first human to step onto the Moon on July 20.

1971—Retired from NASA.

1971 —Professor of aerospace engineering at University
-1979 of Cincinnati.

1978—Awarded Congressional Space Medal of Honor
by President Jimmy Carter.

1979 —Held variety of jobs, including one with a
-1997 consulting company and one with an engineering firm; narrated television specials about
aviation.

1986—Served on government panel investigating
*Challenger* disaster, which killed seven astronauts, including teacher Christa McAuliffe.

1994—Made several appearances at celebrations in
honor of the twenty-fifth anniversary of
*Apollo 11.*

# CHAPTER NOTES

## Chapter 1

1. Edgar Cortright, ed., *Apollo Expeditions to the Moon* (Washington, D.C.: National Aeronautics and Space Administration, 1975), p. 203.

2. Ellen Creager, "Lunar Legacies," *Houston Chronicle*, July 20, 1994, p. A1.

3. Cortright, p. 206.

4. Ibid., p. 209.

5. "A Great Leap for Mankind," *Time*, July 25, 1969, p. 14.

6. Cortright, p. 209.

7. Ibid.

8. Alan Shepard and Deke Slayton, *Moon Shot: The Inside Story of America's Race to the Moon* (Atlanta: Turner Publishing, Inc., 1994), p. 15.

9. Neil Armstrong, "The Moon Had Been Awaiting Us a Long Time," *Life*, August 22, 1969, p. 24.

10. Cortright, p. 212.

## Chapter 2

1. Charles Mortiz, ed., *Current Biography Yearbook, 1969* (New York: H. W. Wilson Co., 1969), p. 18.

2. "Three Men Bound for the Moon," *Life*, July 4, 1969, p. 20.

3. "The Crew: Men Apart," *Time*, July 18, 1969, p. 29.

4. Mortiz, p. 18.

## Chapter 3

1. Alan Shepard and Deke Slayton, *Moon Shot: The Inside Story of America's Race to the Moon* (Atlanta: Turner Publishing, Inc., 1994), p. 62.

2. Ibid., p. 98.

3. Edgar Cortright, ed., *Apollo Expeditions to the Moon* (Washington, D.C.: National Aeronautics and Space Administration, 1975), p. 18.

**Chapter 4**

1. Alan Shepard and Deke Slayton, *Moon Shot: The Inside Story of America's Race to the Moon* (Atlanta: Turner Publishing, Inc., 1994), p. 184.

2. Ibid., p. 185.

3. Ibid., p. 186.

4. "Fire in the Spacecraft," *Newsweek*, February 6, 1967, p. 25.

5. Shepard and Slayton, p. 207.

6. Harry Hurt, *For All Mankind* (New York: Atlantic Monthly Press, 1988), p. 150.

**Chapter 5**

1. Neil Armstrong, "The Moon Had Been Awaiting Us a Long Time," *Life*, August 22, 1969, p. 25.

2. Edgar Cortright, ed., *Apollo Expeditions to the Moon* (Washington, D.C.: National Aeronautics and Space Administration, 1975), p. 215.

3. "A Giant Leap for Mankind," *Time*, July 25, 1969, p. 10.

4. Cortright, p. 216.

5. Alan Shepard and Deke Slayton, *Moon Shot: The Inside Story of America's Race to the Moon* (Atlanta: Turner Publishing, Inc., 1994), p. 246.

6. Cortright, p. 219.

7. Ibid., p. 222.

**Chapter 6**

1. "Greatest Week in the History of the World Since the Creation," *U.S. News & World Report*, August 4, 1969, p. 4.

2. Alan Shepard and Deke Slayton, *Moon Shot: The Inside Story of America's Race to the Moon* (Atlanta: Turner Publishing, Inc., 1994), p. 10.

# GLOSSARY

**abort stage**—Time at which a mission is canceled because of technical problems.

**centrifuge**—A machine that produces artificial gravity by spinning.

**cosmonaut**—A Russian astronaut.

**docking**—Two spacecraft joining together in space.

**g-force**—The force on a person or object caused by a change in acceleration.

**lunar module**—Also called LM—A small spacecraft designed to carry astronauts to the lunar surface from a larger spacecraft.

**microbes**—Organisms capable of causing disease.

**NASA**—National Aeronautics and Space Administration, created in 1958.

**orbit**—The path of one celestial body or artificial satellite around another.

**quarantine**—To isolate those who may have been exposed to contagious diseases.

**reentry**—The act of returning to Earth's atmosphere from space.

**rendezvous**—A meeting, such as when two spacecraft closely approach each other.

**tracking stations**—Sites set up by NASA all around the world to monitor the flight of a spacecraft and to help direct the pilot.

**Tranquility Base**—An area of the lunar surface that was the site of the first Moon landing.

# FURTHER READING

Asimov, Isaac. *Piloted Space Flights.* Milwaukee: Gareth Stevens, Inc., 1990.

Bredeson, Carmen. *Gus Grissom: A Space Biography.* Springfield, N.J.: Enslow Publishers, Inc., 1997.

Cassutt, Michael. *Who's Who In Space.* New York: Macmillan Publishing Co., 1993.

Cole, Michael. *Apollo 11: First Moon Landing.* Springfield, N.J.: Enslow Publishers, Inc., 1995.

Collins, Michael. *Carrying the Fire: An Astronaut's Journey.* New York: Farrar, Straus & Giroux, 1989.

Neal, Valerie, Cathleen Lewis, and Frank Winter. *Spaceflight: A Smithsonian Guide.* New York: Prentice Hall Macmillan, 1995.

Ride, Sally, and Susan Okie. *To Space & Back.* New York: William Morrow & Co., Inc., 1989.

Shepard, Alan, and Deke Slayton. *Moon Shot: The Inside Story of America's Race to the Moon.* Atlanta: Turner Publishing, Inc., 1994.

# INDEX